MW01615436

Unlocking the Secrets of

RETAIL MAGIC

Fourth Printing

August, 2009

Courage Crafters, Inc.

800-290-5028

Unlocking the Secrets of Retail Magic

Copyright © 1998, 2002, 2009 by Richard Fenton and Andrea Waltz

All rights reserved.

ISBN 0-9663981-6-8

Published by

Courage Crafters, Inc.

Originally Published as Accelerated Performance Training

800-290-5028

E-Mail: info@couragecrafters.com

Visit our website at www.couragecrafters.com

My eyes glanced down at the large bouquet of flowers on the passenger seat as I worked my way slowly through the heavy, late-afternoon traffic on Lake Shore Drive, careful not to stop too suddenly. I hoped that Andrea would like what I had chosen.

I reached over to adjust the heat, but accidentally pushed the button for the air conditioning. As the blast of cold air hit my face I quickly remembered back and I thought to myself with a smile... it was exactly a year ago today that our paths first crossed.

Just one year.

One truly amazing year.

PART ONE:

Uncle Edgar's Ugly Gift

It was the day after Christmas, 1979. I threw on my heavy woolen coat and wrapped my scarf tightly around my neck, preparing to brave the bitter winds of Chicago's lakefront for the six-block walk up Michigan Avenue.

Feelings of guilt coursed through me as I called goodbye to my crew and slid out the front door of *ElectroWorld*, the appliance and stereo store I managed for a small but rapidly growing retail chain. This guilt, however, had nothing to do with abandoning my assistant manager who would be staying behind to close up for the night. The store was fully staffed and I felt justified knowing that, like so many managers in the retail business, I had put in my share of 14-hour days during the last six weeks of the holiday season.

No, the guilt I was feeling was simply because I was on my way to return a Christmas gift that came in the mail from Uncle Edgar, never mind that neither my wife Andrea, nor I, could remember having an Uncle named Edgar! We had decided the last thing I needed was another necktie, especially an ugly one, so I was going to return it and use the money to take Andrea out to dinner that evening.

As I made my way through the throngs of bargain hunters and fellow gift-returners, I looked down at the hunter green gift box clutched in my gloved hand. The tan lettering read simply, *The Rag Man, Michigan at Oak,* and I realized that in addition to not remembering an Uncle named Edgar, I also could not recall having ever seen a men's clothing store at that location. I glanced at my watch, which read 4:56 p.m., and picked up my pace. I hoped they would still be open.

Location, Location, Location

To say it was cold outside would have been an understatement as big as the skyscrapers that surrounded me in every direction. I looked at my watch again and saw that I had now been wandering around the intersection of Michigan Avenue and Oak Street, looking for the store in frustration for almost thirty minutes. A typical man in many ways, I wouldn't consider stopping to ask someone for directions, but now enough was enough!

I made my way into the lobby of a corner high-rise and approached the receptionist. "Excuse me," I said politely.

The receptionist looked up and eyed me for a moment, then responded matter-of-factly, pointing, "Elevators at the end of the hall, third level down."

"What?" I said, caught off-guard.

"Rag Man, right?" Her eyes shifted to the gift box still firmly implanted in my gloved hand.

"Uh, yes."

"Well, that's where it is, down in the basement."

In the *basement?* I entered the elevator, pushed the button marked B3 and the doors slid silently closed. Within seconds the doors reopened and I stepped into what could be best described as a typical parking garage, although there was not a single car in sight. It dawned on me that it was 5:30 p.m. on the day after Christmas and most everyone had probably left the building already.

My eyes scanned the garage in every direction, looking for a sign or a display window perhaps, but there was nothing indicating that a store of any kind would be found in this terribly out-of-the-way location.

And then I saw the door.

A plain, wooden door placed oddly in the middle of a barren, gray cement wall. "Could that be it?" I wondered aloud. With no other possibilities in sight, I walked over and reached for the highly polished brass knob.

May I Take Your Overcoat?

Before I could take hold of the knob the door swung open and an immaculately dressed gentleman appeared.

"Welcome to The Rag Man, Mr. Fenton," the man declared with a warm and gracious smile. "My name is Robert DeKoyer and I manage this establishment. Please come in and make yourself comfortable."

As I stepped inside, the beauty of the shop nearly stole my breath. Beautiful oak fixtures held stacks of neatly folded cashmere sweaters and elegant cotton shirts. Rows of pinstriped suits and camelhair sport coats hung from the walls at attention. The light from a large stone fireplace danced in golden flashes on the 12-foot ceiling.

Another sharply dressed salesperson appeared out of nowhere. "May I take your overcoat, sir?" he said.

"Thank you," I managed, somewhat embarrassed at all the attention, "but you don't understand. I'm just here to return a necktie!" My words apparently fell on deaf ears as the salesman and my coat disappeared.

Mr. DeKoyer looked at me. "People enter our store for many reasons, Mr. Fenton. Some come to purchase an entire wardrobe, others a single pair of socks. They wish to have alterations done, exchange items, and like you, they have merchandise to return. Some come to sit by the fire and warm themselves in winter, while others come to cool off during the humid months of our Chicago summers. They come to browse, chat, kill time or," DeKoyer smiled, "to simply have a cup of hot chocolate." At that exact instant DeKoyer placed a large ceramic mug in my hand and I looked down to see that the steaming cocoa was topped with whipped cream, just the way I like it.

"What brings you here is never the point," DeKoyer continued, still smiling.

"What *is* the point?" I asked sheepishly, feeling that I was somehow supposed to know something so obvious.

"That you have chosen to visit *us*, over all the other men's clothing stores in the world you could have gone to, whatever your purpose... *that* is the only thing that matters!"

Joseph, AKA The Rag Man

It was then, for the first time since I entered, that I noticed a group of four or five customers gathered around an elderly gentleman at the rear of the store.

"Who is that?" I asked.

DeKoyer didn't even bother turning to look. "That *is* the Rag Man. His real name is Joseph Crossfield. He started this business many, *many* years ago."

"He must be 80 years old!" I absently blurted.

"Actually, Mr. Crossfield turned 86 just recently, but he has the energy of a man half his age," DeKoyer stated nonchalantly. "He is now retired... well, mostly retired. He loves his customers and his employees and insists on coming in at least one afternoon a week. As you can see, he has a very loyal following."

I watched for several minutes as Joseph Crossfield, AKA the Rag Man, performed his craft. And I also watched the customers who were mesmerized by Joseph's smile and passion and hung on his every word. "You're lucky that you happened in today," DeKoyer added, then offering, "I don't suppose you'd like me to introduce you?" To this day I am not sure why I answered *yes*, but I did, and as we walked towards him, the elderly man's eyes lifted and met mine.

"Joseph, this is Mr. Fenton," DeKoyer announced.

"Yes, I know!" responded the Rag Man, reaching out and warmly shaking my hand. "It's such a pleasure to finally meet you."

"*Finally?*" I asked, bewildered.

"Yes. You are Edgar's nephew, correct?" said the Rag Man with a sly smile. "He talks about you all the time." Then he reached out and took the gift box from my hand and opened it. "Oh, my," he said under his breath, shaking his head slowly from side to side, "This is far too conservative a tie for such a fashion-forward young man. Come with me, I have something incredible to show you!" He turned and headed off, not waiting for my response. And I followed.

* * *

When I made it home later that evening I had some explaining to do, because when I walked out of the Rag Man's store not only did I leave with a replacement necktie, but a brand new shirt to match.

More importantly, however, I also walked out with an invitation. An invitation to have lunch... with the Rag Man.

PART TWO:

Lunch on the Lake

It was two weeks later and I found myself driving my old Chevy through the heart of Lake Forest on Chicago's north shore, one hand on the steering wheel, the other holding directions. I watched the numbers and knew I was getting close when suddenly the most beautiful estate in the neighborhood came into sight. I slowed. This was the place, all right. Unbelievable!

I pulled up to the gate and pushed the intercom button.

"Yes?" a woman's voice said.

"It's Richard Fenton," I responded. "The Rag Man... I mean, *Joseph*, invited me to lunch."

The gates swung open and I drove about a quarter mile to the front of the house. As I mounted the steps the front door swung open and an elegant woman in her mid-seventies appeared.

"Please come in," she said with a smile that made her immediately likeable. "My name is Anika Crossfield, but everyone simply calls me Annie. Joseph is in the study, the last door on the left," she said, pointing down a hallway that looked like it had no end. "Lunch will be ready soon."

* * *

I called his name several times, peering into the empty room, when finally a glass door in the far wall of the study swung open and the Rag Man appeared with an enormous cigar in his left hand.

"Richard!" he called out. "How are you, my boy? You know, it's been one of my dreams for years to have a walk-in, and on Christmas morning Anika surprised me with *this!*" He motioned to the closet-sized humidor, and as he did I could detect tears of pride and joy welling up in his eyes. "Quite a girl, my Annie," he said, reaching into his pocket for a monogrammed handkerchief. He dabbed his eyes, then looked at me and smiled. "You met her, I presume?"

"Oh, yes, she's wonderful!" I replied in earnest.

"A good start!" he proclaimed. "We agree on something already!" He reached into the desk drawer and searched around for several seconds. "Ah! Matches!" he exclaimed, quickly walking from behind the desk and sliding past me and through the office door. "I never smoke in the house," he called to me over his shoulder, already halfway down the hall, "What do you say we take a walk?"

Caterpillars in the Greenhouse

After a long walk, we finally reached a door that led out to a small greenhouse. It seemed surreal, the two of us standing in a dome of warmth with the wind and snow swirling on the other side of the glass, the frozen lake not more than a hundred feet away.

He clipped the end of his cigar and lit it. "So, Richard, do you work hard?"

"Well, sure. I mean, *I am in retail.*"

He laughed hard. "Yes, that was a silly question! Let me rephrase it this way… Are you as productive as you could be?"

"Some days I am," I said shrugging.

"And what is it that keeps you from being your most productive on the other days?" he inquired.

I thought hard, feeling tested, then answered, "Time, I guess. There never seems to be enough time to accomplish everything I want."

The Rag Man turned on his heels and said, "I want to show you something." On a small wooden table sat a large glass jar. He lifted the lid and reached in. When he turned around I could see that he held several caterpillars in his hand. "Watch this," he said. He placed one of the caterpillars on the edge of a small flower pot, then another caterpillar directly behind the first. He continued this until the entire rim of the flowerpot was filled with caterpillars.

"These are called *processionary* caterpillars," he stated, "getting their name because they follow one another in…"

"A procession?" I broke in.

He smiled and seemed pleased that I was following. He reached down and grabbed what looked like dried grass from a metal bucket that was sitting on the floor. "Pine needles!" he declared, "The favorite food of the processionary caterpillars." He placed a large handful of the needles in the center of the flowerpot.

"Now, tell me Richard, would you say these caterpillars are busy?" the Rag Man asked. I watched as they moved in circles around the rim of the flowerpot, one after the other, in a steady rhythm.

"Yes," I replied.

"They want the pine needles, but they are ignoring them. Is their inability to reach their goal due to lack of time?"

"No."

"Then what is the problem?"

"They're not using their time properly."

"Exactly. To be a successful manager the first thing you need to understand is that the very concept of time management is ludicrous! *You can not manage time, you can only manage activities… what you do with your time.* Even with their favorite food mere inches away, these caterpillars will continue to follow each other like this for days, until they will literally die of starvation and exhaustion, and for one simple reason; because they are confusing *activity* with *accomplishment*. They think that because they are moving they are getting somewhere, but clearly they are not. However, with a little redirection…"

He reached down and placed his finger on the edge of the flowerpot, breaking the procession and directing one of the caterpillars toward the center of the pot. Immediately the others followed and within seconds they all began feasting on pine needles.

"Most managers do not need more time to be more successful, Richard, what they need is a little *redirection. **Always keep your eye on your activities, not on your watch!*** " Then he looked down at his wrist and said, "Speaking of watches, mine says it's time for lunch."

The Favor

We sat and relaxed in the kitchen, sipping apple cider as Anika moved about the kitchen, cooking up a storm. Finally, I said, "I was very impressed with your store, and I really want to become an excellent manager. Will you teach me?"

"Well," he said in a somewhat coy manner, "the most important ingredient for a teacher is a willing student. We would have to get together several times, three at a minimum. I could never begin to cover everything in a single afternoon."

"That's no problem!" I replied as Anika placed a large plate of noodles smothered in white cream sauce on the table. "I'm willing to do whatever it takes."

"Whatever it takes?" he asked, raising an eyebrow.

"Yes."

"Okay, then it's a deal, providing…."

"Providing…?" I asked quizzically.

"Something simple, a small favor. Agreed?"

Whatever the favor was, I was willing to do it. I nodded silently, yes. His eyes danced with delight and I realized he was just as excited to share his secrets with me as I was to learn what he knew. He smiled a big smile, dug his fork into his fettuccini and took a large mouth full, then he exclaimed, "Annie! This is the best Alfredo you've ever made!" The Rag Man's wife looked at me and winked, as if to say she'd heard it a thousand times before. I knew, of course, that she had.

And I also knew that every time Joseph said it, that he meant it with all his heart.

PART THREE:

Let's Play Two!

It was early April, almost three months since I had lunch at the house, and I had just about given up on getting together with the Rag Man. I was sitting at my desk, wadding through stacks of paperwork and daily transaction reports, when I noticed a cream colored envelop with neither a stamp nor a return address. I opened it and out spilled a single ticket to the Cubs home opener… a box seat right behind third base! Also enclosed was a handwritten note that read, *Richard: I trust you can get the afternoon off. Meet me at the park at 11:00 a.m. Joseph.*

* * *

The usher pointed me toward my seat and I could see Joseph was already there, a box of popcorn in one hand and a scorecard in the other. I called out, "What on earth can I possibly learn about winning at a Cubs game?"

The Rag Man turned and smiled. "Oh, you'd be surprised! Have a seat, my boy, the lesson's already started." I took my seat and realized that even though I love baseball it had been at least five years since I'd made it out to Wrigley.

"You follow the Cubs, Richard?" the Rag Man asked.

"Used to," I replied as my mind was instantly transported back to the summer of '69 when I would ditch school with my friends and sneak into the ballpark. Heck, I still knew the starting line-up by heart: Kessinger, Beckert, Williams, Santo, and Ernie Banks, Mr. Cub, a man who loved the game so much that his motto was, 'Let's play two!' because he wanted everyday to be a double-header.

"Do you always come out early for batting and infield practice?" I asked. It was, after all, only eleven o'clock in the morning and the actual game didn't start until 1:00!

"This is when the real work is done," he said.

"I agree. I've always felt the game was won or lost in practice," I responded.

"Good," he said with a smile. "I see that I don't need to sell you on the importance of coaching and development, so let's get right to today's lesson."

I reached into my jacket pocket for my notepad but he stopped me. "No need to take notes," the Rag Man said, holding up a small leather book with his initials engraved in gold letters on the cover, "I've got it all written down right here! So, are you ready?"

"Yes."

"Good. Look at the field and tell me what you see."

The Dodgers were on the field taking batting practice. "I see players warming up, practicing, and I see coaches drilling them on the basics and providing feedback on their performance."

"Good. What else?"

I searched the entire ballpark for whatever it was that I was obviously missing. Finally giving up I said, "Nothing. That's all I see."

"Let me give you a hint," Joseph said, handing me the scorecard and the sports section from the Sun Times.

The Best Get Better

I sat there, sports pages in hand, and watched the Dodgers finish batting practice. Then infield practice. I was just about to throw in the towel when something struck me. I opened the sports page and reviewed the player statistics for the entire Dodger team. "I've got it," I declared with a big grin.

"Tell me."

"The key is not *that* the coaches are coaching, it's *who* the coaches are coaching! The players with the best batting averages and the best fielding percentages are getting most of the attention. It's the opposite of what you'd expect."

"Exactly!" he said beaming. "One of the most important decisions facing a manager is deciding which associates they should invest the majority of their coaching, training and developmental time with. Unfortunately the majority of managers make the wrong decision. Tell me, Richard, how many sales people do you have working for you at *ElectroWorld*?"

"Nine or ten," I said.

"Let's say ten, it makes the math easier!" he chuckled. "If all things were equal, each associate would do 10% of the store's total sales."

"All things are never equal in retail," I replied.

"Of course they aren't. I'd guess that you have at least one superstar who does more than their share, probably 15-20% of the sales, am I right?"

"17% to be exact," I replied.

"You know your numbers, that's good! And you've probably got about another four above average associates doing maybe 12% of the store's total volume apiece, give or take. What does that come to?"

I quickly added in pencil on my scorecard. "65 percent," I answered.

"Okay. So if the top five associates account for 65% of the sales, that would leave 35% to be split between the bottom five associates, about 7% each."

"Yes," I confirmed.

"So, who do you spend most of your time with, Richard, the top five... or the bottom five?" the Rag Man asked. I didn't need to respond because my face said it all.

"The fatal mistake that most managers make," he continued, "is directing most of their efforts to the bottom half of their team in the belief that this group presents the greatest opportunity for overall store sales improvement. Nothing could be further from the truth! Whom would you rather get a 10% improvement from, a ballplayer who is hitting .300, or a player hitting .240? Or, in retail sales terms, an associate doing $5,000 a week or someone at $3,000?"

"Are you suggesting not to bother coaching and developing the bottom half at all?"

"Certainly not, but the time you invest in them should be significantly less than the amount of time you spend with your top performers. Always remember this... it is the associates on the low end of the performance ladder that are the least likely to change. And, there are other benefits that happen when you focus attention on the top half. Retention of above average performers increases dramatically. Excellent people often quit jobs because they don't feel they are growing - more developmental attention reduces this problem. You know what we do at my store?"

"What?"

"We have some special training programs we put people into, but you have to be in the top half in terms of performance to get in! Our people learn quickly that training is a reward you earn by performing, not just a tool to improve performance. You'd be amazed at how this motivates people to battle their way into the top half to qualify."

"So the best keep getting better," I said.

"Yes, and when the best keep getting better, watch out- because the sky is the limit!"

The HIT List

Joseph pulled out a cigar and stuck it between his still perfect teeth and then lit it. "Where were we?" he said, "Oh, yes, the hit list!"

"The *hit* list?" I replied, "That sounds dangerous!"

"It is dangerous... dangerous if you don't make one and stick to it!" he laughed. "In addition to focusing development on the *right people*, it's critical to focus on the *right skills*. That's where the hit list comes in. H.I.T. is an acronym I made up – it stands for High Impact Training."

"Wouldn't there be a different list for each associate, depending on their individual needs?" I asked.

"No!" he said emphatically. "Just because someone has a low level of competence in a given skill, that doesn't mean the competency should be developed."

"Are you suggesting some skills *never* get developed?" I asked.

"Not at the expense of high-impact skills that *must* be developed they don't! A manager must decide which skills really make a difference and then focus on those skills with a passion."

"How do I know what goes on the H.I.T. list?" I asked.

"Simple," he said, "when you think of an area of development, just ask yourself if being better at this skill will have a direct, immediate and profound effect on sales and customer service. If you can answer *yes*, with conviction, then it goes on the list."

"For example?"

"Okay, which of these items would have the most direct, immediate and profound benefits to you and your customers: Teaching your people how to effectively manage sales objections, or teaching them how to handle customer complaints?"

"They both sound important to me." I responded.

"Perhaps, but consider this… the opportunity to manage an objection happens with almost every customer, but the opportunity to handle an upset customer is, hopefully, a rare occasion. To have maximum impact on sales and customer service you must weigh the impact of every coaching and training activity you engage in.

The toughest decisions for managers are not about what *to* do but rather what activities to *minimize*. *There is never enough time to get to everything, so don't do everything- do the right things!* Don't become one of the caterpillars mistaking activity for accomplishment!"

The *Response-Able* Salesperson

"Let's go back to the topic of managing objections again; see that woman over there eating the orange?" the Rag Man asked, pointing.

"Yes," I replied.

"Well, imagine if you squeezed that orange... what would come out?"

"Orange juice," I said shrugging.

"Yes. But *why*, when you squeeze an orange, does orange juice come out?"

"Because that's what's inside?" I replied, my response sounding more like a question than an answer.

"Good. Now, does it matter what time of day you squeeze? Does it matter if you squeeze the orange with your hands or with some sort of device? No! When you squeeze an orange, orange juice comes out... *because that's what's inside.*"

I thought to myself, what on earth does squeezing oranges have to do with managing objections? "I don't really get where this is going," I admitted aloud.

"Simple. Imagine a customer asking the price of an item and the salesperson responds, *$400*. The customer says, *$400! You must be out of your mind! That's an outrageous price for that!* How might a salesperson feel at that moment?"

"Attacked... nervous... pressured." I guess.

"*Squeezed*?" The Rag Man added.

"Yes! Squeezed!"

"So," the Rag Man continued, "when you squeeze a *salesperson*, what is going to come out?"

"Whatever is inside!"

"Exactly! Good answers, bad answers, or no answer at all... that is what will come out! How a salesperson responds when under pressure, when squeezed, is determined well in advance of that moment. If they're unprepared, they will falter. Managers must put the good stuff inside so that when they're squeezed, your people will be *response-able... able to respond!* If you don't put it in, it can *never* come out!

"Certain skills like managing objections, transitioning from a single unit to additional merchandise, asking a closing question to help the customer make a decision... these are skills that remain largely under-developed for most salespeople, even though they have massive impact on sales and customer service. Your H.I.T. list must include items like this, and everything else must wait until these skills are fully developed. To quote Gerta, *'The things which matter the most must never be at the mercy of the things which matter the least!' "*

And with that, Joseph stood up and walked off to stand in the long lines that had formed at the restrooms.

Build Your People...

The starting lineups were announced with great opening-day fanfare and the Cubbies took the field as thirty-nine thousand hometown fans cheered with optimism that this would be the year the pennant drought would end. The optimism was short-lived, however, as the first batter walked, the next man up singled, and then Steve Garvey promptly parked a hanging curveball on Waveland Avenue. Some things never change.

"Did I miss anything?" Joseph asked, returning to his seat.

"Three runs, two hits for LA," I moaned. We ate dogs and crunched on bags of peanuts for several innings and eventually the conversation turned back to business.

"So, Richard, are you a good salesperson?" the Rag Man asked.

"Right now I am probably the best salesperson I've got," I said with pride, suddenly realizing that my answer didn't make me look very good in terms of hiring and developing salespeople.

"Then it must be very tempting to spend a lot of your time with customers, correct?"

"Tempting? It's all I do! 80% of my time is spent on the floor selling."

"So," he asked, "while you are taking care of the *external* customer, who's developing your *internal* customers? Your associates?"

"The time I spend with customers *is* part of my team's development," I protested.

"And how is that?" he inquired.

"When I'm selling I am modeling the way!"

"Oh, I see. And what exactly are your people doing while you are, how did you put it, *modeling*?"

"Well, they're taking care of customers, too."

He leveled his serious brown eyes at me. "This may not be what you believe, Richard, but it's a fact: When everyone is with a customer, there is no development happening. *Either you have to be watching the associate do their job and then providing them with immediate feedback, or they must be observing you as you as you model the way, and then providing you with feedback.* Someone has to be without a customer for development to be taking place."

"I understand what you're saying, Joseph, but we're just too busy most of the time. I don't have many non-productive hours to spend on associate development."

"Did you hear what you just said, Richard? Do you really consider time spent on associate development to be *non-*

productive! If you do, it's no wonder you're not getting the results you want!"

"That's what my company calls hours which are not spent directly taking care of the customer, for things like meetings and training," I said defensively. "I didn't create the term!"

"Regardless of the term being used, it's the mindset that matters! *The most productive hours you spend are one-on-one with your people, training and developing and coaching them.*"

"But every customer I spend time with increases the level of service for that customer!" I declared.

"And every salesperson you don't spend time with *decreases* the level of service to five or ten other customers," he responded flatly. "Management is unique because your worth is not determined by your direct effort but rather the collective effort of others. If you go to work every day believing that the way to increase overall team effectiveness is by personally taking care of as many customers as possible, then you'll never reach the top level of management performance."

The Rag Man pointed to the field. "Is there any doubt about the influence Tommy Lasorda has on the results the Dodgers get? Of course not, yet he doesn't personally hit or field! All of his results come through the development and the performance of his team. *If you truly want to touch as many customers as possible you must do so through your people. Build your people... and they will build the business!*"

26

Dull Gray Walls

The score was seven to three, the Dodgers still on top, and the organ player pounded out an enthusiastic version of *Take Me Out To The Ballgame* during the seventh inning stretch. When we sat back down the Rag Man said, "Let me tell you another story. I once worked as the men's wear manager for a large department store not far from here. The general manager came to me late one afternoon and said that the president of the company was flying in from Dallas to visit the very next morning! He wanted me to round up some volunteers to work late, staying overnight if necessary, to make sure the store was perfect. We worked like mad until five in the morning, folding sweaters, polishing fixtures and even doing some painting.

"At 9 o'clock sharp the president arrived. The general manager said, 'Let me take you on a tour of the store, Sir.' The president replied, 'Fine, but why don't we start with the lunchroom!'

"Well, we all walked down to the lunchroom and the president glanced around at the dull gray walls, the empty snack machine, the dirty tables, and then slowly shook his head. The general manager finally broke the silence, asking, 'Are you ready for a tour of the sales floor now?' to which the president responded flatly, *'There is no need for the rest of the tour. I know everything I need to know about your store already,'* and then he turned around and left."

"You mean he flew a thousand miles, looked at the lunchroom for five minutes, and left?" I asked in disbelief.

"Yep! And I never forgot it. I learned that day that as a manager you work for your people. Even though they *report* to you, y*ou* work for *them!* It's a manager's responsibility to provide the training and the tools and the environment people need to be successful. *If you want to get the most from your people, you must give them as much attention as you do the ultimate customer, and then amazing things will happen.*"

Opportunity, Means and *Motive*

Bill Russell came to the plate for the Dodgers to start the top of the ninth with Cubs still trailing by four runs. "Since you love baseball, Richard, can I assume you were excited when you got the ticket for the game today?" the Rag Man inquired.

"Yes!" I replied, "And thank you. By the way, how did you know I liked baseball?"

"Your Uncle Edgar, of course," he said. Once again I was too embarrassed to admit I still could not remember Uncle Edgar. Then he asked, "How do you motivate people at ElectroWorld?"

"I don't have to do much in terms of motivation," I replied.

"How's that?"

"Our people are on commission and that provides everyone with the same motivation. Money!"

"Money is great motivator, Richard, but it's not the only motivator. Actually, most research today shows that money is fairly low when workers are asked what's important to them. Would you say the ticket to the game today was part of your motivation to meet with me?"

"Sure," I admitted.

"What if, however, I were trying to motivate your wife, Andrea. Would tickets to a Cubs game be the way to do it?" he asked.

"She's not crazy about baseball," I responded, "but an invitation to Sunday brunch, now that would get her excited!"

"Motivating *different* people with *different* desires but using the *same* reward doesn't make sense, and it usually doesn't work. Do you ever watch any of the cop shows on TV?"

"Not too often, they're all pretty much the same."

"I know what you mean. They all start with detectives standing over a dead body when a car pulls up and out gets the star of the series. He asks, 'What have we got?' One of the other detectives responds, 'Female, 38, shot in the heart. The husband's inside being questioned. He definitely had opportunity and means to commit the crime, but we're still unsure of the….'" the Rag Man's words trailed off as he looked to me to finish the sentence.

"… Motive?" I offered.

"Yes, or in other words, the *reason*. Just as customers are motivated to buy for their reasons, not ours, sales associates are motivated to sell for their own reasons. To motivate people you must know their motives, or what *drives* each individual. Somehow we've come to believe that *one reason fits all*. Well, it doesn't!

"I have no doubt that some of your people are motivated to be their best just for the money, but others require different forms motivation... Having you write a letter about their performance and forwarding a copy to the district manager... Being kept in the loop about what's happening in the organization... Being invited to a management meeting to show them their opinions matter... Getting called to the office and finding out it's not because they did something wrong, but rather something right... Discovering a post-it note stuck to their time card that says simply, *Nice job yesterday!* Your people will be thinking about small acts like this long after their paycheck has come and gone."

"Basic recognition," I said.

"Yes. As Napoleon said, 'I am always amazed that soldiers will march into battle and die for nothing but a simple ribbon.' "

"What about sales contests?" I asked. "You're not going to tell me *they* don't work, are you?"

"No, but contests do lose impact when you have too many of them. Why not, when you have your next contest, try making the prizes more personal, something other than cash. Cash is about as personal as giving your wife a gift certificate for Valentine's Day! *The most memorable gifts are the ones that require the most thought, so why not create contests that have maximum impact by making the prizes personal?"*

"Are you suggesting a different prize for each person?"

"Sure. At the end of the last contest we had at The Rag Man, Tom won two tickets to a Bulls game, Bill got a day off to spend with his daughter, and Sue won the opera glasses she'd been wanting to buy for months."

"That's a lot of work, finding out what motivates each person. Who's got the time?"

"Hopefully you do, Richard, because that's what it takes to become a master motivator. Once you begin to work harder at finding out what motivates each person on your team the most ironic thing will happen. You're people will try harder than ever, not to win the contest necessarily, but because they enjoy working for someone who would take the time to get to know them as people."

As the final batter for the Dodgers popped up to the shortstop the Rag Man stood up and stretched, then said, "That's it for me today."

"But the Cubs still get their last ups, it's not over yet."

"Oh, yes it is," he replied. "To use your words from earlier, the game is won in practice."

PART FOUR:

It's All Happening at the Zoo

It was the middle of July on what was perhaps the hottest day of the year. I had just walked into the store after helping a customer load a television into the back of their station wagon when my assistant manager told me I had a phone call.

"Richard, my boy!" the voice exclaimed, "Do you have plans for lunch?" It was the Rag Man.

"Uh, no, not really," I said.

"Good! What do you say we meet at the Lincoln Park Zoo, around one o'clock?"

"The zoo?" I asked quizzically.

"Yes, the zoo! They have a new African lion exhibit that just opened and I thought it would be a good place for your next lesson."

"Sure, this is a great day for a safari!" I said sarcastically, wiping sweat from my forehead.

"Great. I'll see you at one."

* * *

I sat on a concrete bench in front of the lion exhibit, thinking how much I'd be willing to pay for even the slightest breeze, when Joseph arrived wearing a camelhair sport jacket and brown wool slacks.

"How can you wear a sport coat on a day like this, Joseph," I moaned. "It's got to be 102 degrees!"

"Today is my day at the store. I'm heading over there after we're done with lunch. Speaking of lunch," he said, holding up several brown paper bags with big oil spots on them, "I picked up some sandwiches on the way here. You do like Italian sausage, right?"

"I better, I live in Chicago!" I replied with a laugh.

We unwrapped our sandwiches and took big bites, enjoying the flavor of the food and watching the animals watch us in return.

"Let me start by asking you a question, Richard. What is the single most important task of a manager?"

I was excited because I knew the answer to this one. "To make a profit!" I replied with confidence.

"Profit is a good thing, but profit is the *result* of excellent management, not a management task. This might seem like semantics, but I assure you it is not. Try again."

I thought hard before answering, then finally said, "To coach and develop my people and to challenge them to succeed."

"Extremely close." he said with a smile. "With the exception of a single word I'd say you were exactly right. Perhaps the best way to make my point is for me to tell you another story."

Go For No!

The Rag Man leaned back, pulled out a cigar and lit it. "My first job in sales was for a chain of men's stores, in Boston. The district manager, a man by the name of Harold, was in one afternoon and I really needed to impress him. I was brand new and I wasn't really setting the world on fire. Quite honestly, I was worried that if my sales didn't improve that they were going to let me go. This is right at the time that I was courting Anika, and her father didn't think to highly of me anyway," Joseph said laughing and slapping my leg, "and the last thing I needed was to suddenly be without a job!

"Well, I get my first 'up' and in walks a finely-dressed gentleman who tells me he wants to buy an entire wardrobe of clothing! Within minutes I have the biggest sale of my new career and I was feeling mighty proud of myself. I was sure that Harold, who was watching from not too far away, would be impressed.

"After the customer left, Harold finally sauntered over. 'Nice sale, kid', Harold said to me.

"My chest puffed out with pride. $400! I proclaimed. This was back in 1937, mind you, when $400 was a lot of money! Anyway, Harold just stood there not appearing overly impressed, then he said, 'I'm just curious, but what did the customer say *no* to?' What do you mean? I shot back, that guy just bought a suit, a sport coat, three shirts, six ties, shoes, socks, a belt and underwear!

"Harold waited for me to quit defending myself, then said, 'We've already established what he said yes to, Joseph. What I want to know now is, what did he say *no* to?'

"I thought for a long time, mentally reviewing the sale in my mind, then sheepishly I said, *nothing*. 'So,' Harold asked, 'Then how did you know he was done?'

"His simple question hit me like a punch because I realized the customer hadn't ended the sale, I had! Why? For only one reason I could think of... because the customer had hit *my* spending limit. You see, I had never spent over $400 on anything in my life, so when anyone went over *my mental spending limit...* hey, *they* were done!

"Harold said, 'The salesperson never decides when the sale is over, the customer does. The salesperson should never beat the customer to the register!' Then he looked me straight in the eye and said, 'Joseph, your fear of hearing the word *no* is the only thing standing between you and greatness.'

"It was amazing! I had gone to work that morning hoping to keep my job. I went home that night knowing I was only two letters away from greatness. And the letters were N-O."

Fail Your Way To Success

"When I asked earlier you what a manager's most important task was, Richard, you said to challenge your people to succeed more. My experience with Harold taught me that really

35

great managers do just the opposite... they challenge their people to fail more!"

"Help them to *fail* more?"

"Yes. Not to become failures, but to increase their *rate of failure*, and in the process increase their ultimate *rate of success*."

"I give my people pep talks all the time, telling them not to be afraid of customers," I responded, "but it doesn't seem to make any difference, at least not with most of them."

"That's because you're taking the approach most managers take, which goes something like this..." He took the bag his sandwich came in, flattened it, and drew this diagram:

ATTITUDE → BEHAVIOR → RESULTS → RECOGNITION

"Most managers believe that to get better results from salespeople you need to change their attitudes, then they will change their behavior and get better results. Then the manager runs over and recognizes them when they succeed. Sound familiar?"

"Yes, that's what I've been taught."

"Well, forget it! That only works when the associate is already highly motivated to change, which is less than 10% of the time."

"So what does work?"

"Quite simply, this!" Under the first diagram he wrote the same four words, but this time in a different order:

BEHAVIOR → RECOGNITION → RESULTS → ATTITUDE

"The best way to get behavior change is to change behavior," the Rag Man said.

"That statement makes no sense!" I responded.

"Believing that preaching at people will cause them to alter their behavior, that's what makes no sense! *To get behavior change, lasting behavior change, you must make someone try something new, and when they experience the results of the new behavior, that will change their attitude.*"

You Can't Make 'Em Drink!

"That sounds good in theory, but how do you force someone to try something? I mean, you can lead a horse to water…" I mumbled.

"Ah!" the Rag Man responded, "what a great analogy! How *would* a horse respond to each approach? Using the first method, you'd tell the horse all about how great water is and hope this would get the horse excited (attitude), then all on his own he'd go over and take a drink (behavior), he'd no longer be thirsty (result), then you'd give him a sugar cube for reinforcement (recognition)."

"Yes, that's a fair analogy." I said.

"Well, I'm suggesting that if you want to get consistent behavior change from people, the way to do it is to drag the horse to the water and make him take a drink (behavior), reward him immediately with a sugar cube just for trying (recognition), he'd feel refreshed (result) and suddenly realize, *Wow! This water is great stuff!* (attitude).

"This is your advice, *dragging* people?" I asked in disbelief.

"Metaphorically speaking, absolutely! Your most important task as a manager is to challenge people. I'm talking about dragging them, kicking and screaming if necessary, to show them how good they could be if they would only try! I've tried both methods and the second is the only way to get results, not just with horses, but also with people."

"So you're saying to reward people not only for the results they get, but also for the effort?"

"And for risking failure and rejection. It's imperative that managers not only recognize people for their successes, but also for their failures. After Harold shared his insight about my obvious fear of hearing the word 'no', he reinforced my behavior change on every store visit by congratulating me not just for the *yes's* I received, but also for the *no's* I collected."

The Rag Man was right! We do run over to congratulate our salespeople for the big sales, for their successes, but how many times do we congratulate someone for the sale they missed; when they showed tremendous courage by trying but came away with nothing but a series of *no's*?

If A Man Wears Socks…

"I remember one time when a complaint letter came to my attention at the store," the Rag Man continued. "This gentleman said he'd bought over $3,000 in clothing from Tom, one of our top salespeople. He went on to say that after spending that much money in my store that Tom had the audacity to try and sell him socks!

"I gave the letter to my general manager, Robert. I believe you met him. Anyway, I wanted to see what he would do about it."

"And…"

"Robert called the customer and asked him to tell his story, then he inquired directly if Tom had been rude or discourteous in any way. The customer said, 'No, Tom was very polite but he just didn't take no for an answer very easily!' So Robert suggested the customer come by the store and pick out some socks on us of course, then asked the customer jokingly, 'You do wear socks, don't you?' The customer said, 'Of course I do!' "

"So what did Robert do then, with Tom I mean."

"He did exactly what a great manager should do. When Tom came in for his shift the next day, he found a neatly gift-wrapped box on the counter with his name on it. Inside were three things… a copy of the complaint letter from the customer, a dozen pair of socks worth about $100, and finally a note which read, *Great job, Tom! If a man wears socks, sell him socks! -Robert.*"

"How did Tom react?"

"Exactly the way Robert had expected. Tom immediately became the top sock and accessory salesperson in the store."

"Wow! Wasn't Robert worried that Tom would get the wrong message and think that customer service wasn't important?"

"Oh," the Rag Man said, raising his eyebrows, "You're one of those!"

"One of those *what*?" I demanded indignantly.

"One of those people who believes that selling and customer service are somehow separate, that you have to make a decision to choose one or the other. Let me share a concept with you that will make a big difference in the way you manage. Do you still have some time?"

"You bet!"

"Good. There are five types of salespeople, Richard, but only two that you want to have working for you. I asked you to join me at the zoo because it's the perfect place for me to explain this concept, but before I get too deeply into the animal kingdom, I need to tell you another story."

The Pickled Patron

"A few years back, I think it was 1949 or so, I was lucky enough to land a position as the training director for a large department store in Los Angeles. They took a big chance on me because I had no prior training experience, at least nothing formal.

"My first assignment was to create a sales training program. The project was due in two days and all I had completed so far was the title! At lunch I went across the street to a small coffee shop for food and inspiration, and that's exactly what I found.

"I was sitting at my table with a yellow note pad with nothing but the words *What makes a salesperson great?* written across the top, when suddenly I heard a voice say, 'I know what makes a salesperson great.' I knew it wasn't God because the voice was coming from the booth behind me. I spun around and there sat a very inebriated man in tattered and dirty clothing. I'm sorry, I said, we're you talking to me? The disheveled man pointed to my notepad and repeated, 'I know what makes a salesperson great!' I thought to myself, what could it hurt? I was getting nowhere on my own, so I decided to listen.

"His definition caught me completely off guard. 'A great salesperson is someone who makes you happy!' he stated in precise though somewhat slurred words. I sat there, shocked at the simplicity but also at the depth of his answer. The next thing you know Robbie, that was his name, is sitting at my table and I'm buying him lunch. He basically wrote my training program for me!"

"And it was a great success I'll bet!"

"No, it wasn't! Turns out he was only half-right."

"How can someone be *half-right*?"

"Well, before Robbie started hitting the bottle he had a job as an insurance salesman. His company gave him some clients to manage and they loved him. He worked very hard to make them extremely happy, so in that regard, he was right. The problem was that Robbie was deathly afraid of appearing pushy, so he never got around to the other half of what makes a salesperson great... which is to actually sell something! Eventually the company fired him. It turned out that Robbie was a Retriever!"

"Did you say... a *Retriever?*"

"Yep. A very nice, extremely likeable, Golden Retriever."

The Retail Jungle

"Let me show you what I mean," the Rag Man said as he flipped the already flattened paper bag over and began drawing once again. "The behavior of salespeople is determined by two key factors..."

HIGH

CONCERN for MAKING FRIENDS!

RETRIEVERS | LIONS!

OTTERS

HIPPOS | SHARKS

LOW

CONCERN for
MAKING the SALE!

HIGH

"One factor, shown on the left side of the diagram, is the salesperson's level of concern for *making friends*, from low on the bottom to high on the top. The other factor, shown across the bottom, is the salesperson's level of concern with *making the sale*, from low on the left to high on the right. Every salesperson can be plotted on this matrix, and the result is five distinct selling styles. Understanding this simple concept will help you in every aspect of management, from recruiting and hiring, to coaching, training and motivating."

Lions and Retrievers and Sharks, Oh My!

"The first style is what I call the Retriever," the Rag Man began.

"Robbie," I confirmed.

"Yes, Robbie was a Retriever. Robbie had a high concern for making friends and being liked by the customer, but low concern for making the sale. Everyone loves Retrievers because they are kind and gentle; they are into feelings and creating a bond with others. Their number one priority is to make sure that people like them, and as a result, they are perceived as good with customers. The problem with Retrievers is that they are so afraid of upsetting a customer they rarely sell to their potential. Their selling style is fairly passive. Do you have any sales associates like this?"

"Too many," I responded.

44

"The opposite of Retrievers, over here on the bottom right, are the Sharks."

"I've got a few of those working for me too!" I laughed.

"Sharks have a high concern for making the sale, but a low concern for making friends. Their style is aggressive and they often take a hard-sell approach with customers. They rarely bother to ask questions or determine needs, and if they do ask questions they don't listen to the answers! Sharks troll the waters of the retail sales floor looking for their next meal... I mean sale! They are the kind of salespeople who throw merchandise in front of people without finding out anything about them, then pile on the sales pressure until the customer screams, Uncle! The only two things that matter to Sharks are, *Did the customer buy?* and *How much?*

"Down here," the Rag Man said, placing his finger on the lower left corner of the diagram, "you've got the Hippos. Hippos don't care if they are liked *or* make the sale! A Hippo's major concern is if the paychecks have come in yet. You can usually tell Hippos the minute you walk into a store because they're the ones camped out somewhere near the cash wrap, holding up the counter in case of an earthquake. Hippos sell with apathy; they place merchandise before the customer and it either sells or it doesn't, and then they think, *"Hey, I get paid just the same... is this a great job or what!* Hippos are far more interested in base pay than commissions, contests or bonuses because they know they'll never qualify for performance based rewards. They sneak into companies because of managers who don't do their job during the screening process."

"I don't have a single Hippo working for me!" I said with pride.

"I'd be very disappointed if you did," the Rag Man replied. "Right here in the middle are the Otters. Otters are hard working and industrious people who show up on time, follow directions and achieve moderate sales goals. They are part-Shark in that they show some concern for making the sale, and part-Retriever because they do have some concern for being liked by customers. The sales floors of the best retailers in America are populated primarily with Otters, but Otters are only about half the way up the sales and service food chain. The problem is that Otters, as good as they are, are somewhat reactive and process-oriented with customers. They do not take charge as fully as they should. One of your primary tasks as a manager is to develop Otters into..."

"Into *what*? I asked expectantly.

Running with the Lions!

"... LIONS!" he said emphatically. "Unlike Sharks who manipulate customers for their own benefit, or Retrievers who are afraid to manage an objection or trade a customer up, or Otters whose sales approach is good but not always proactive, Lions are assertive and *in control* without being aggressive or *controlling*.

Webster's defines *control* as the 'power to direct', and that's what Lions do… they direct! Lions are assertive enough to create large multiple-sales and confident enough to dissuade a customer from a color or model that is inappropriate. Lions are the king of the retail jungle because they understand the greatest secret of all…"

"Which is?"

"*…To sell is to serve!* When you shop at a store that employs Lions you can instantly tell the difference! Annie has a favorite boutique she takes me to over on Rush street. When she's in the dressing room the salespeople automatically bring her skirts, blouses and accessories by the armload, saying in a polite and cheerful voice, 'Here, Mrs. Crossfield, why don't you try this on too!' And what do we call that? We call it great service, but it's also great selling! Lions believe that *to not sell* a customer merchandise that fills their needs *is a disservice!*"

"My salespeople say they're are afraid of pushing too hard, of accidentally stepping over the line," I admitted.

"Most salespeople have mentally backed so far away from the line they don't even know where the line is anymore! The only way anyone can know if they are selling to their potential is if, every so often, they get a little resistance. And if they *do* step over the line with a customer they can just pull their toe back to safety, but in the process they will have discovered just how great they can really be. In that moment they will be *running with the lions!"*

He stood and brushed crumbs from his lap and handed me the paper sack with his hand-drawn diagram. And with that, the Rag Man turned and headed off to work to deliver a level of sales and service to his customers, which at that stage of my retail management career, I could only dream of.

PART FIVE:
A Walk in the Woods

It was a Friday evening late in October. I had stopped off at the supermarket to pick up some groceries when I spotted a pumpkin stand and decided to surprise Andrea by getting the biggest one I could find.

As I made my way up the stairs to our apartment with the monstrous pumpkin under my arm I wondered how I was ever going to get my key in the door. At that moment the door swung open and there stood Andrea with a big grin. "Anika and Joseph Crossfield invited us to join them for brunch this Sunday at the Herrington!" she yelped with delight.

The Herrington is a small but exquisite hotel nestled along the Fox River in the quaint town of Geneva, Illinois, about 50 miles west of Chicago. And, by coincidence, it just happened to be the place Andrea and I had spent the first night of our honeymoon.

48

"I already said yes," Andrea added, leaving no room for negotiation and instantly proving Joseph's earlier lesson in motivation!

* * *

On Sunday morning we all arrived at the hotel at exactly the same time. Joseph pulled his Lincoln Continental gracefully into the parking space next to mine. Still driving at the age of eighty-six, or perhaps eighty-seven by now I thought, realizing I had known Joseph for almost a year but had never discovered when his birthday was. It wouldn't be long before I found out.

"We wanted the two of you to join us this morning," Anika said immediately after we were seated, "to celebrate Joseph's birthday!"

"Why didn't you tell us?" Andrea exclaimed. "We would have brought a gift!"

"That's exactly why my dear," Joseph added, "and, besides, Richard still owes me a favor. I'll consider that to be my birthday gift!"

I had almost forgotten about the favor, but it was obvious that Joseph was not going to.

Don't Hire Seeds, Hire Trees!

After stuffing ourselves silly with crabmeat omelets, bacon and fresh fruit, Joseph suggested the two of us go for a walk while we let our "ladies" have a chance to get to know each other.

"So what's new at the electronics store?" he asked as we made our way along a shaded path which wound through tall oak and maple trees.

"I'm finally in the running for a district manager position," I said with a smile. "The interview is next week."

"I'm glad," he said, "And don't worry... I have a feeling you'll get it, and I know you'll do a superb job. But first there are still a few things we need to cover. Tell me, what is the fastest way to develop an entire team of peak performers?"

"Well, everything we've talked about, I guess. Coaching, role playing, lots of one-on-one development."

"Good. I don't want to minimize anything we've already covered, but I also want you to consider this: *The quickest way to get someone up to speed is to hire someone who is already up to speed. Or, in other words, the most effective training strategy you can have is to avoid the need for training in the first place.* If your goal is to move people from *Level A* to *Level Z* in terms of development, would you rather start with an associate who's at *Level A,* or *Level Q?* When you hire superstars at the outset you're automatically 90% of the way there!"

"That sounds real good, Joseph, and maybe you get some great applicants at The Rag Man, but apparently you haven't seen the people coming into my store to apply for jobs! The lions are working for someone else already!"

"That's exactly right! The best people *are* all working for someone else already, Richard, so if you are ever going to have a store filled with lions you must identify and surgically remove them from their current place of employment and transplant them into yours. If recruiting is not a *major* element in your overall associate development plan then you will never reach the top of the management mountain."

"I've tried recruiting but it's never worked for me," I said.

"Nothing worthwhile is ever easy, Richard," the Rag Man said, bending over to pick up a large acorn. "Learning to recruit effectively takes time and consistent effort, but if you stick with it the rewards are immeasurable. You have to decide if you want to hire this..." he said as he placed the acorn into the palm of my hand, "or this!" He moved his arm in a sweeping motion toward the tall trees that surrounded us. *"Don't hire seeds... hire trees!"*

You Are Your Standards

It felt great to walk off the food we had eaten. Finally we came to a bridge built specifically for trains to cross the river. We rested there for several minutes before turning back.

"I have some final thoughts I want to share with you, Richard, before we finish our last session together," the Rag Man said.

"Our last session?" I asked.

51

"Yes. I've already shared the basics of what you need to know, except perhaps the most important thing, which has to do with the standards you set.

"When someone knocks on the front door of your house, do you simply swing the door open and let them in without looking first? No. In today's world we need to be careful whom we let in... into our house, into our life, and into our company. When applicants come knocking at your door, don't just swing it open. *Great managers find ways to bring more applicants to the door, but they make the door hard to open. Great managers don't just let anyone in.*"

Skill vs. Will

"I remember a sales associate named Keith who worked for me several years ago. After three months Keith had settled in to the middle-of-the-pack, never the top salesperson, and never the bottom. He would come in about a half-hour early every day, get a cup of coffee, glance through the paper, organize his personal-trade files and relax before we unlocked the doors for business. Well, one morning I walked in and I could tell instantly there was something going on with Keith. He was on fire! He was busy brushing suits and straightening shirts, moving with a sense of urgency I had never seen in him before.

"When the store opened he paced the floor, keeping his eye on the front door like the Prize Patrol was going to arrive with a check for $10 million dollars! I couldn't imagine what had gotten into him. Finally, a man walked in and Keith waved excitedly, yelling across the store, 'Over here, Dad, over here!' So that was it! Keith's father had come in to see where Keith worked and to buy some clothing. Suddenly it all came together! The suits Keith had brushed earlier were the 42 longs, the size his father wore... the shirts he was straightening were his dad's size, 16 ½ by 33.

"Keith took his dad on a tour of the store, including the tailor shop, then proceeded to sell him clothing like a salesman possessed with enthusiasm and passion. Finally, he escorted his father to the door, shook his hand firmly and told him how much he looked forward to his next visit. Everything he did was perfect!"

"Then what?"

"Keith meandered to the rear of the store, poured himself the cup of coffee he had forgotten earlier, and took a sip. He played with his personal trade files for a bit, and then when I pointed out a customer who had slipped through the front door without being greeted, Keith casually walked up and said in a friendly but flat tone, 'May I help you?' The fire was gone, and Keith had once again become... *Keith*. But for one magical moment I had the chance to see the *lion* in him.

"What did you do?"

"Once I knew what Keith was capable of I began to expect his best everyday, with every customer, but Keith was unwilling to deliver it. Notice that I didn't say he was *unable* to deliver it, but *unwilling.* If it were a matter of skill we would have invested more time trying to coach and develop him, but it wasn't a lack of *skill,* it was a lack of *will.*"

"So you let him go?"

"There is no room in your store for a single associate who won't treat every customer like they were family, and to the degree that you allow such people to take up positions on your team you define yourself as a manager. Keith left on his own because he began to feel uncomfortable in his job once we demanded his best everyday. He ended up taking a position with another retailer down the street who gladly accepted the average level of service Keith was willing to deliver."

Yes, the perfect place for an average performer *is* working for the competition I thought to myself. Then just as quickly another thought struck me; a year ago I would have been content with an entire staff of average performers like Keith, but now my standards were quite different. How far I had come already!

"Last weekend Annie and I went to Las Vegas," the Rag Man continued, "to see that Irish dance thing, you know…"

"Lord of the Dance?" I offered.

"Yes! Lord of the Dance. You know why I decided to take her to see it?"

I shrugged.

"Because six months ago I saw Michael Flatley being interviewed on television. The interviewer asked him why he gave so much of himself in every performance. Flatley said, 'People come from hundreds of miles to see the show. They don't want to know that I'm 39 years old. They don't want to know that at the end of the night I have to ice my legs. All they know is that they want tonight to be the best show of my life. Not tomorrow night... tonight!'

"It's people like that, people with the hearts of lions, that I want working for me. I'll accept nothing less... and neither should you."

We walked through the clearing and headed back toward the hotel, his final words still ringing in my ears, as in the distance we could see *our ladies* who were at the riverbank feeding the throngs of ducks and geese which had also come out for Sunday brunch.

PART SIX:

A Year to the Day

It was December 26th 1980, exactly one year to the day that my path first crossed with that of the Rag Man. What a great year it had been... and I knew the best was yet to come.

We had learned earlier in the day that Andrea was pregnant, about six weeks along! I took her to her favorite restaurant for dinner, jokingly asking the maitre d' for a table for three. Then we spent the rest of the evening excitedly going through books of baby names. We had just decided on Walker Scott if it were a boy, and Jena Kay if a girl, when the phone rang.

I said, "You get it, it's probably your mom!" We had left a message on her mother's answering machine earlier asking to call us that evening.

Andrea calmly said hello, trying to conceal the excitement in her voice. She went silent for what seemed like forever before saying softly, "I'm so sorry... yes... I'll tell him." She placed the receiver down and turned toward me, the blood gone from her face.

"What is it?" I asked fearfully.

"Honey," she said slowly, pausing and fighting back tears, "That was Anika. She wanted to let us know... that Joseph died last night. The funeral is Saturday."

A Sea of Friends

My eyes glanced down at the large bouquet of flowers on the passenger seat as I worked my way slowly through the heavy, late-afternoon traffic on Lake Shore Drive, careful not to stop too suddenly. I hoped that Andrea would like what I had chosen.

I reached over to adjust the heat but accidentally pushed the button for the air conditioning. As the blast of cold air hit my face I quickly remembered back to the day I searched in the freezing cold for the store. As sad as I felt about his passing, I also felt a great deal of happiness for having known him at all.

The promotion to district manager that I wanted so badly had finally happened due in no small part to the lessons he had shared. And as an extra bonus, the position came with a company car. Maybe not the car of my dreams, but a big step up from the old Nova.

I pulled into the driveway and tapped the horn lightly, shifting the flowers to the back seat as Andrea made her way down the frozen walk. On the long drive to the cemetery, neither of us said a word. But as I turned through the gates, Andrea gasped, "Richard, look at all these people!" A sea of friends, customers and acquaintances, over a thousand people in all, had turned out in zero degree temperatures to say goodbye to Joseph Crossfield, a man who sold clothing for a living.

Amazing.

After the graveside service had ended, we made our way through the throngs of people to where Anika graciously received a long line of well-wishers offering condolences or sharing stories of how her husband had touched their lives.

When our turn finally came, Anika smiled and kissed Andrea on the cheek, then reached out and touched my hand. Leaning forward she whispered, "You were one of his favorites," then she added, "Oh, I almost forgot! Joseph left something for you at the store, something to do with a favor. He said you'd know what that meant."

Tarnished Brass

On Monday during lunch I went over to pick up whatever Joseph had left for me. I walked quickly through the parking garage to the entrance of the store and reached for the doorknob… but it wouldn't turn. Why would the door be locked on the middle of a Monday afternoon? I lifted my hand to knock and then froze - the once beautiful oak suddenly looked old and worn, and the brass knob, which was kept polished and gleaming at Joseph's insistence, was dirty and tarnished.

What on earth was going on?

Perplexed, I took the elevator to the lobby and made my way to the information desk, relieved to see the same receptionist from a year ago. "Excuse me," I said as she concentrated intently on the most recent issue of *People*. "I was just in the garage, down on B3, and for some reason The Rag Man appears to be closed."

"The rag *what?*" she responded, puzzled.

"The Rag Man. You know, the store in the basement. You directed me to it the last time I was here."

"I'm sorry, sir, but there is no store in this building by that name. Besides, why would anyone put a store in the basement?" she laughed, shaking her head and going back to her magazine.

I walked in a daze over to the building directory and ran my fingers over the R's. No Rag Man. Then, as I turned to leave the words Management Office caught my eye. Surely they would know what was going on.

The desk at the management office was deserted, the receptionist most likely at lunch, but I could hear a voice coming from a nearby office and within seconds a man appeared.

"How can I help you?" the man asked.

"Is the property manager here?"

"That's me. Tom Kirkland." He reached out and shook my hand. I took a deep breath. "Mr. Kirkland, I'm a customer of the men's clothing store that's in the basement of the building, The Rag Man. Do you know the store I'm talking about?"

"In the basement you say? Where exactly?"

"On the third level of the parking garage. The entrance is a brown door in the middle of the wall. There is no sign."

"Oh, I know where you mean. On the east wall, right?"

"Yes! The east wall!" Thank God.

"Sure, I know the location. Used to be a clothing store there, at least that's what I've been told, but that was years ago!"

"Years?" I stammered.

"There hasn't been anything in there since the turn of the century. Heck, I've shown the space a few times but never been lucky enough to get a tenant. Not down there!"

My heart sank. Could this really be happening? "I don't suppose you could let me see the space? I wouldn't take long."

"Sure, why not. I can't begin to guess what condition it's in, but if you don't care...?"

"That's fine."

"Hang on, I know there's a key somewhere..."

The Favor *(revisited)*

Kirkland turned the key in the antique lock and the door swung open, then he switched on his flashlight. "No juice, not in here," he said. He moved the beam of light around the room. "So, you say you shopped in here for clothing, huh? Look familiar?"

My eyes scanned the room. The racks, where fine suits once hung, still lined the walls but now held nothing but cobwebs. Kirkland waved his flashlight through the darkness and there was the large brick fireplace, still occupying its place on the back wall of the store. Then I turned to my right, and just as I expected, there was the cash wrap... dusty and untouched for almost a hundred years. "Yes," I responded flatly, "It's just the way I remember it."

As Kirkland turned and headed for the door, something caught my eye... a small black book lying on the counter near where the cash register had once been. "Hey, I hate to rush you," Kirkland called, "but I've got a two o'clock appointment."

"I'm coming," I replied, quickly sliding the book into the pocket of my suit coat.

"You find what you were looking for in there?" Kirkland asked as he locked the door behind us.

"I think so. Thank you."

"No problem," he said. He shook my hand again and then walked off toward the elevators.

* * *

I waited until the elevator doors slid closed behind him before hurrying to remove the book from my pocket. I brushed away the thick layer of dust and saw the initials "JC" in faded gold. Then, slowly, I opened the book. There on the inside of the front cover, was a handwritten message. It read simply:

Richard: I asked you once for a small favor, and here it is. Take what you've learned, and share it with others.

And it was signed...

The Rag Man

About the Authors...

RICHARD FENTON is President of Courage Crafters, Inc. and a professional speaker, sales and management trainer with a specialty in the retail industry. As the story goes, Rich gave his first paid speech at the age of eight! *"I took plastic dinosaurs and set them up on a table in my basement, then invited everyone in the neighborhood over to hear me talk about them. As I recall, I charged 5 cents per person to get in!"* That was over 30 years ago, and Rich has been speaking and training ever since. He has held the position of Training Director for some of America's most prestigious retailers, including ***Macy's, Hart, Shaffner & Marx,*** and ***LensCrafters.*** Richard is a member of the National Speakers Association. His sales, coaching and recruiting programs have been used to train tens of thousands of retail leaders, managers and sales associates all across the US and Canada.

ANDREA WALTZ is the co-founder of Courage Crafters, Inc. She started her retail career as a sales associate with ***Hallmark*** while finishing school at Long Beach State University in Southern California. In 1993 she accepted a position with the world's largest retailer of eyeglasses, ***LensCrafters,*** where she quickly moved through the ranks, becoming one of the youngest managers in the company's history. Her stay also included a stint in the training department where she *got the bug* to teach and develop others. She was the Director of Training for Centinela Pet Supplies based in Los Angeles CA. Along with Richard she is the co-author of "The Run with the Lions Sales Safari" and "Go for No!" Together, Richard and Andrea have created programs and conducted workshops for Tommy Hilfiger, Genesco, Build-A-Bear Workshop, Coldwater Creek, Pep Boys, and many more.

Extraordinary Programs for World Class Retailers...

Driving Sales Performance:
Challenge Your People to be Their Best

Because a manager's worth is not determined by direct effort, but rather the collective effort of others, *Driving Sales Performance* takes a strategic approach to accelerating retail performance. Participants are challenged to use the critical thinking skills necessary in today's results oriented retail environment to propel their team to achieve peak levels of performance. Designed for frontline store managers, field managers and trainers.

Run with the LIONS

Sales training has never been this much fun... *or this effective!* Participants learn to identify the critical success behaviors of top retail salespeople and explore methods for developing and mastering these highly effective sales and service skills. Including a wide variety of skill-building exercises and role-play activities, this program was designed for all retail associates regardless of skill level. Highly recommended for frontline managers to improve ability to coach and develop sales associates and to better identify peak performers during the interview and recruiting process.

S·Y·S·T·E·M·A·T·I·C
RECRUITING

Systematic Recruiting teaches participants a *step-by-step*, proven method to help successfully identify, contact and surgically remove top performers from their current positions and transplant them into your organization. Employing a mix of presentation, exercises and role-play, *Systematic Recruiting* is a must for keeping pace in the highly competitive race to capture your share of the ever-dwindling supply of top talent. Designed for frontline managers, field managers and HR personnel.

To book a Richard and Andrea for a keynote presentation or workshop, call 800.290.5028 or www.fentonwaltz.com

Other Books and Materials...

Go for No!

Yes is the Destination , No is How You Get There

Twenty-eight year old copier salesman Eric James Bratton is about to learn a very important lesson. And he's going to learn it from the most unlikely of mentors - himself! Imagine going to bed one night, then to awaken the next morning in a strange house with no idea of how you got there. Only this house doesn't belong to just anyone – it belongs to you... a wildly successful future version of the person you might one day become, providing you are willing to start doing one simple thing. The lessons Eric learns are destined to change the way he thinks, the way he sells, and the way he lives, forever. And they'll do the same for you! $12. 80 pages. Visit www.goforno.com

The Run with Lions Sales Safari

A Self-Paced Skill Development Book Designed
Specifically for Retail Sales Associates

Send your salespeople on a training expedition without ever having them leave the store! This is a self-paced, fun, and different approach that makes everyone who learns the concepts want to become a "Lion," the "King of the Retail Jungle!" Program materials include: a 64-page book formatted around 10 skill development "expeditions" from "Greeting" to "Adding On to the Sale" and optional items: Self-Assessment Quiz and Leader's Guide for managers. For more information on the Sales Safari, visit www.fentonwaltz.com.To order, call 800-290-5028.

PLUCK!

Providing Courageous, Take-Charge Retail Service
(and having your customers love you for it!)

On a typical overcast San Francisco morning, 20 year old Sarah McIntyre attends her first day of orientation at Winthrop's Department Store just off the city's historic Union Square. But when she accidentally finds a torn and tattered training manual in a dress department fitting room, Sarah is magically transported 100 years in the past! And while she's there, Sarah will learn the secrets of memorable, passionate service from the ultimate source – the company's founder, the legendary B.L. Winthrop! $8.95 64 pages.

To order additional copies of any of our books,
please call 800-290-5028. Quantity discounts available.